OWL-MAZING

FANTASTICAL COLOURING FOR OWL LOVERS

I created this book for all my Owl illustration loving friends
- old & new!

My owl drawings are most definitely not true to life and
are meant to be coloured any colour you like. So the idea while
colouring this book is to relax and have fun.

Don't get precious just let go. Think like you did when you were 7.

OWL-MAZING - Fantastical Colouring for Owl Lovers © 2019 Angelea Van Dam

SWATCH YOUR COLOURS

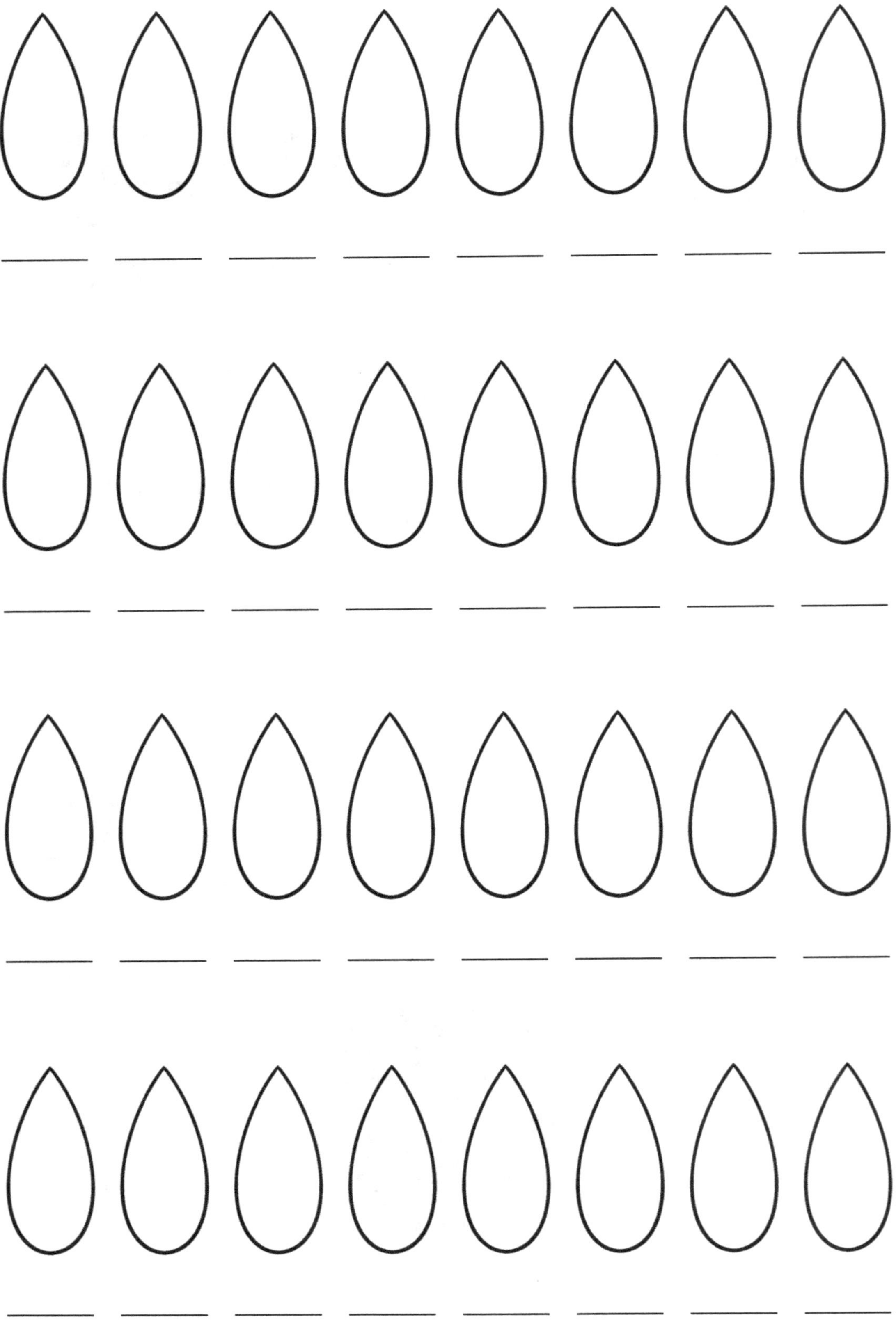

SWATCH YOUR COLOURS

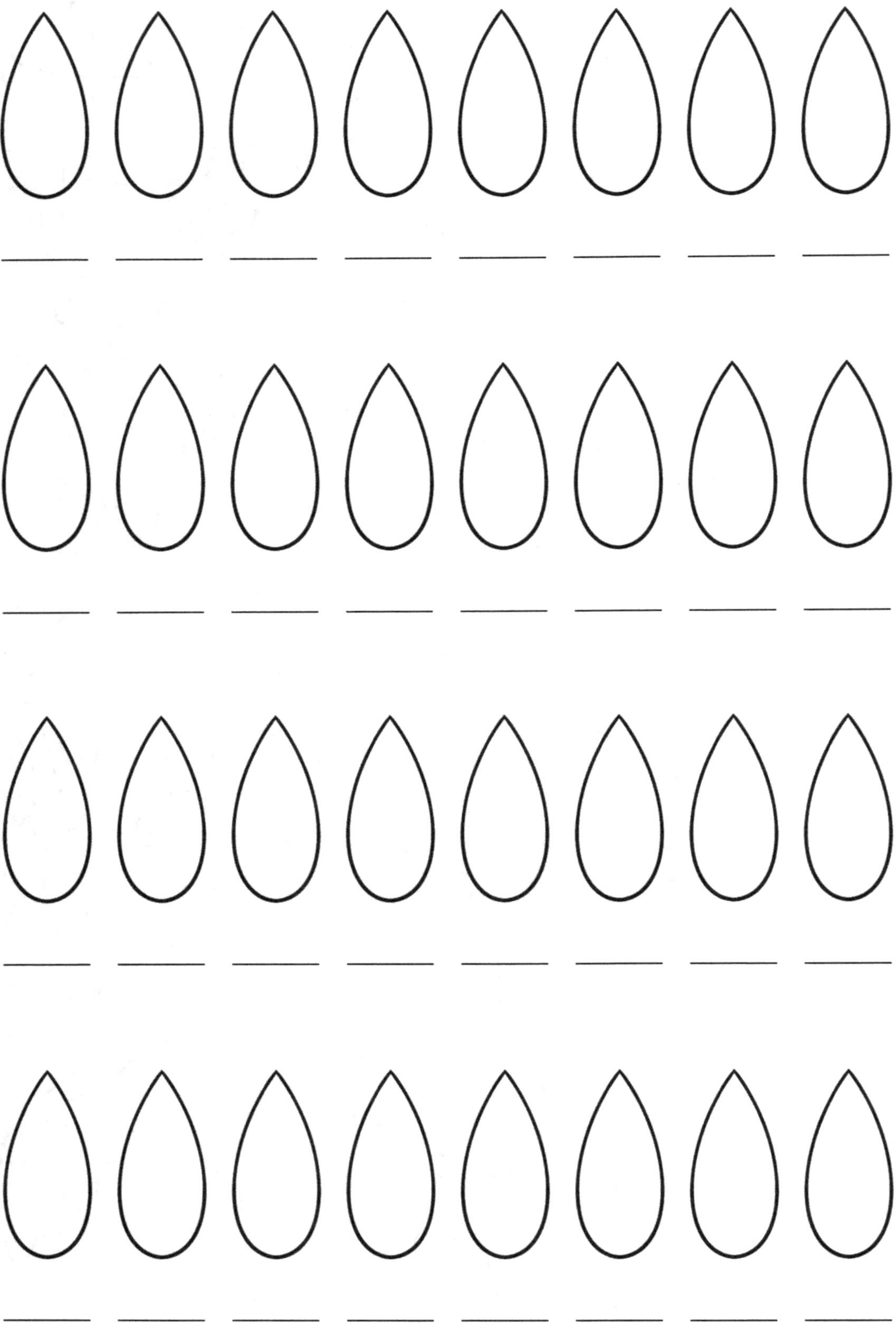

SWATCH YOUR COLOURS

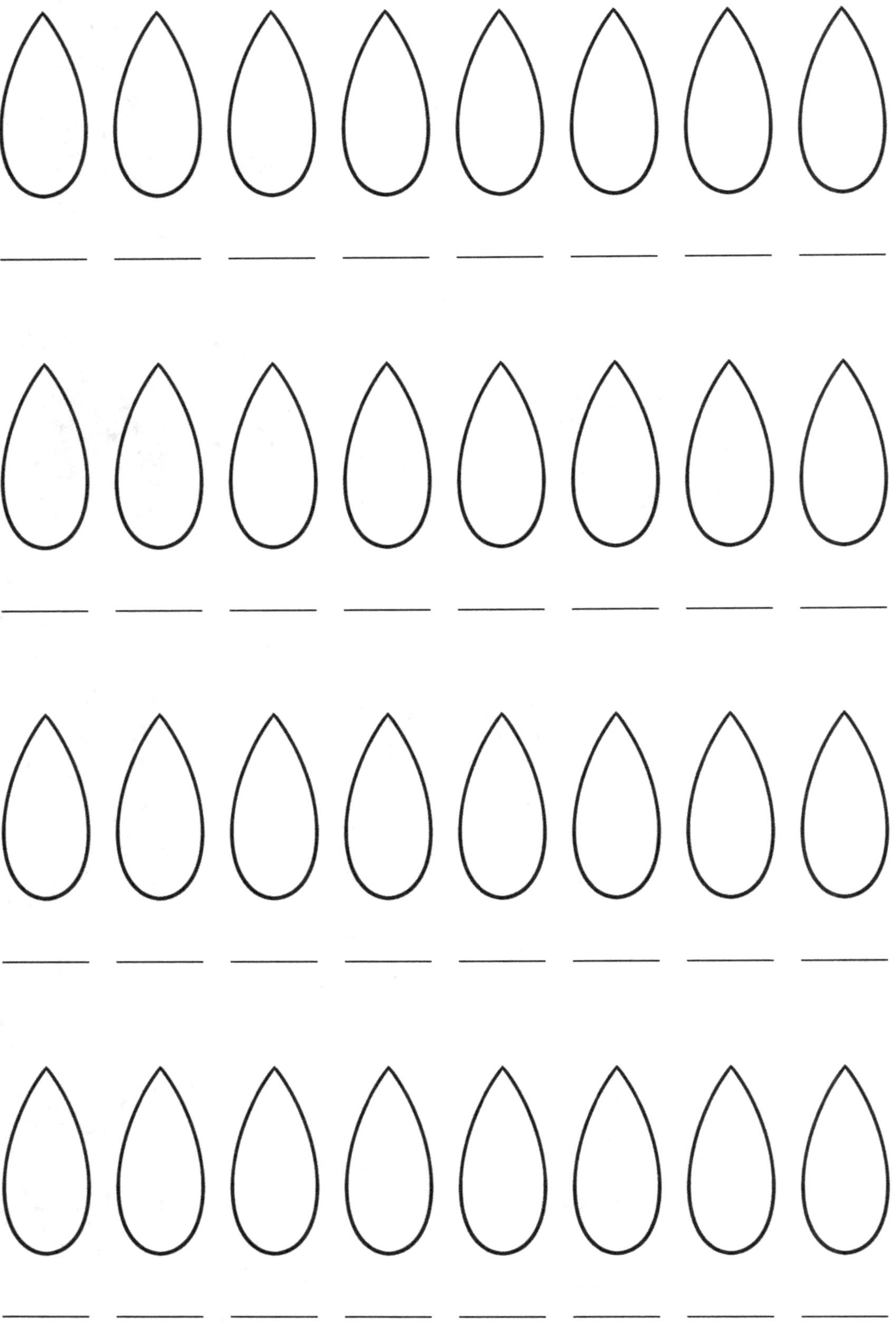

SWATCH YOUR COLOURS

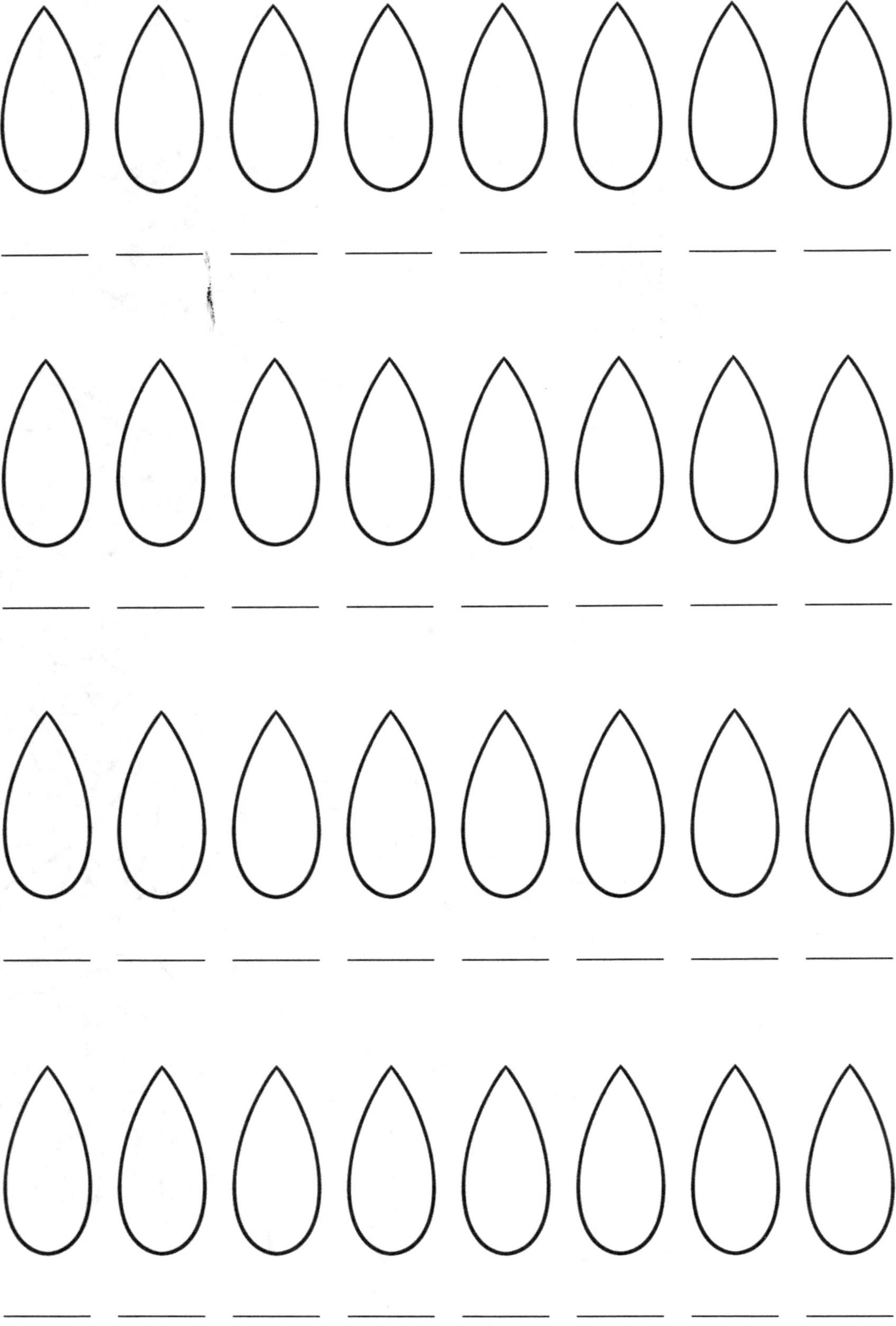

SWATCH YOUR COLOURS

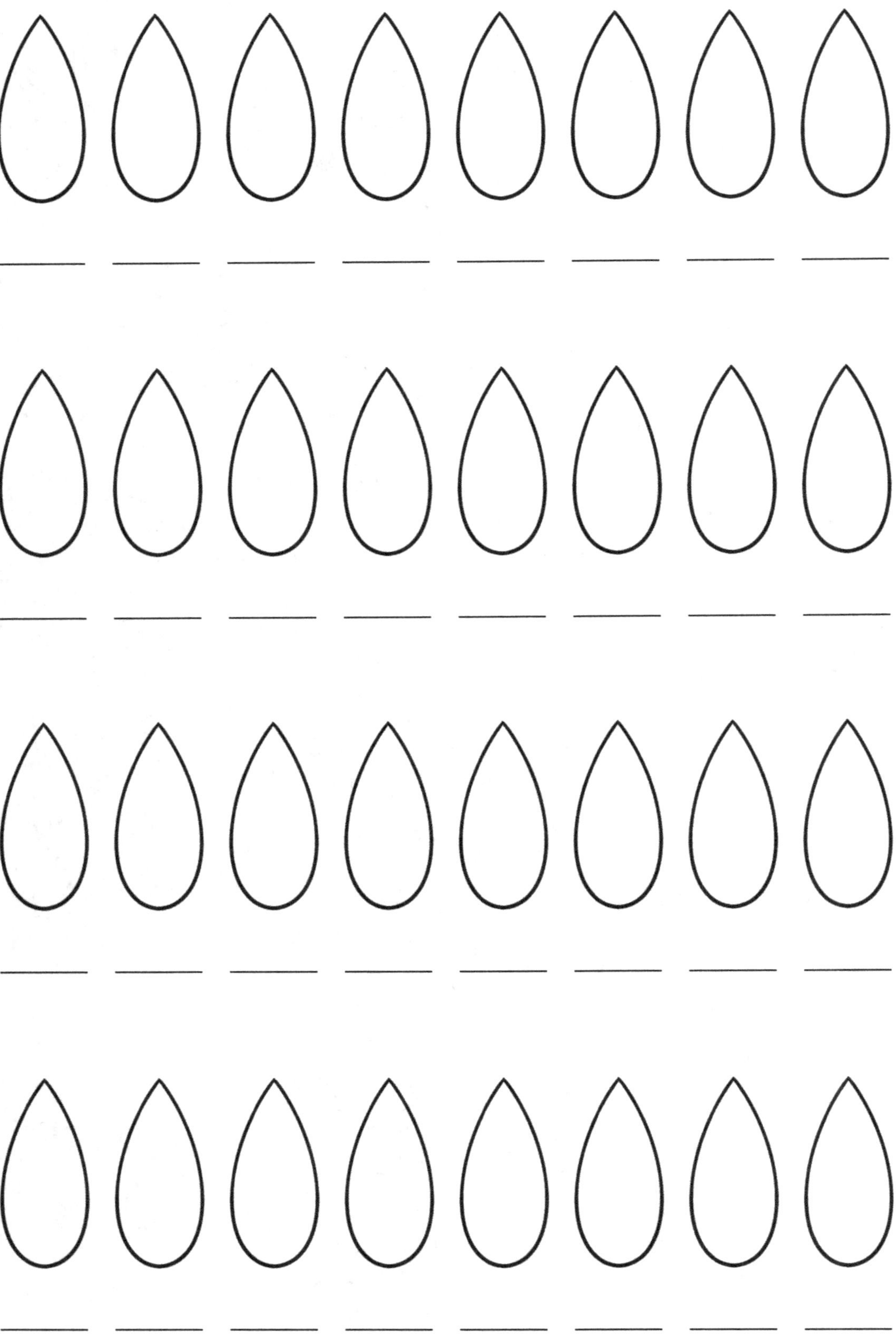

SWATCH YOUR COLOURS

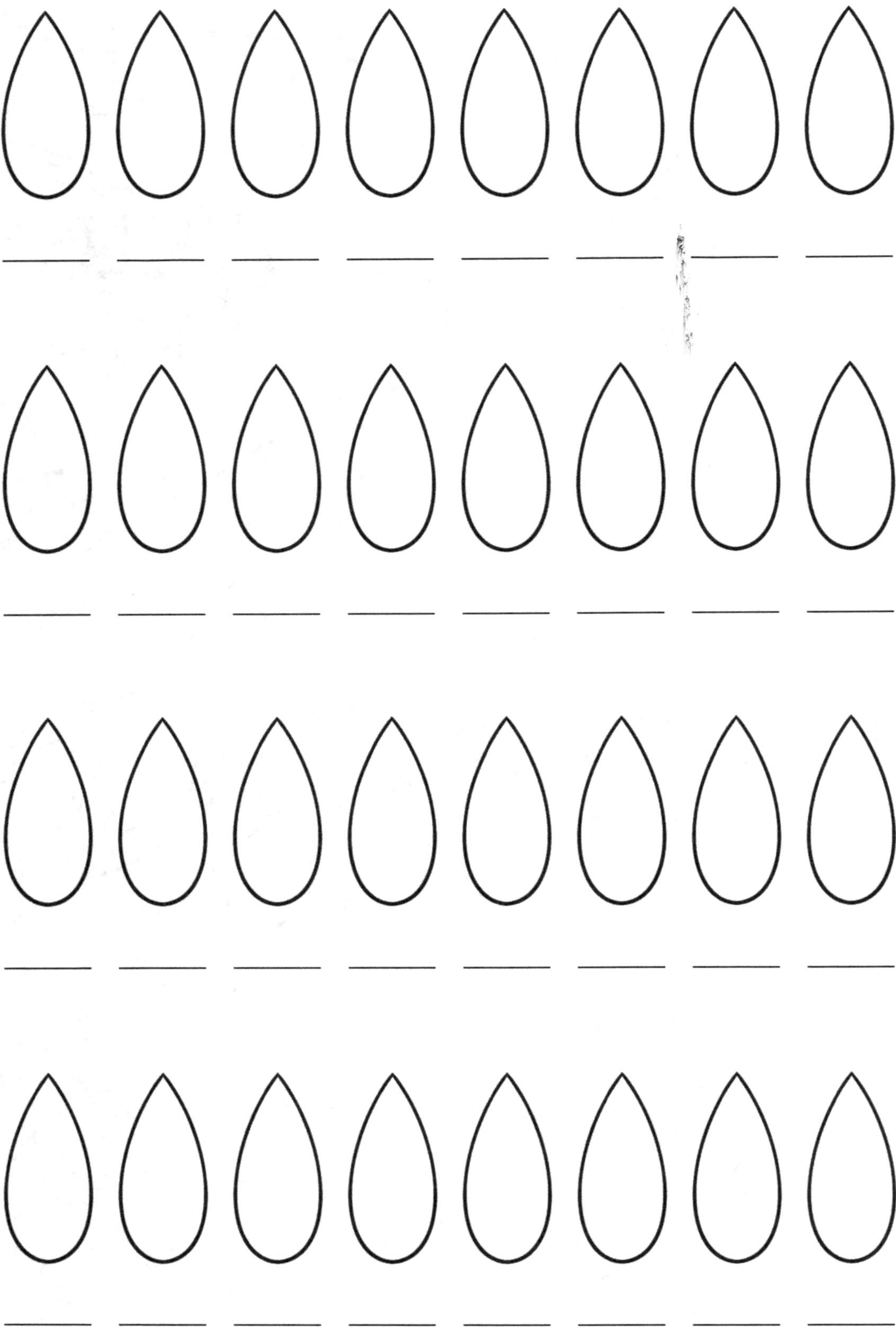

SWATCH YOUR COLOURS

HOOT!!

SWATCH YOUR COLOURS

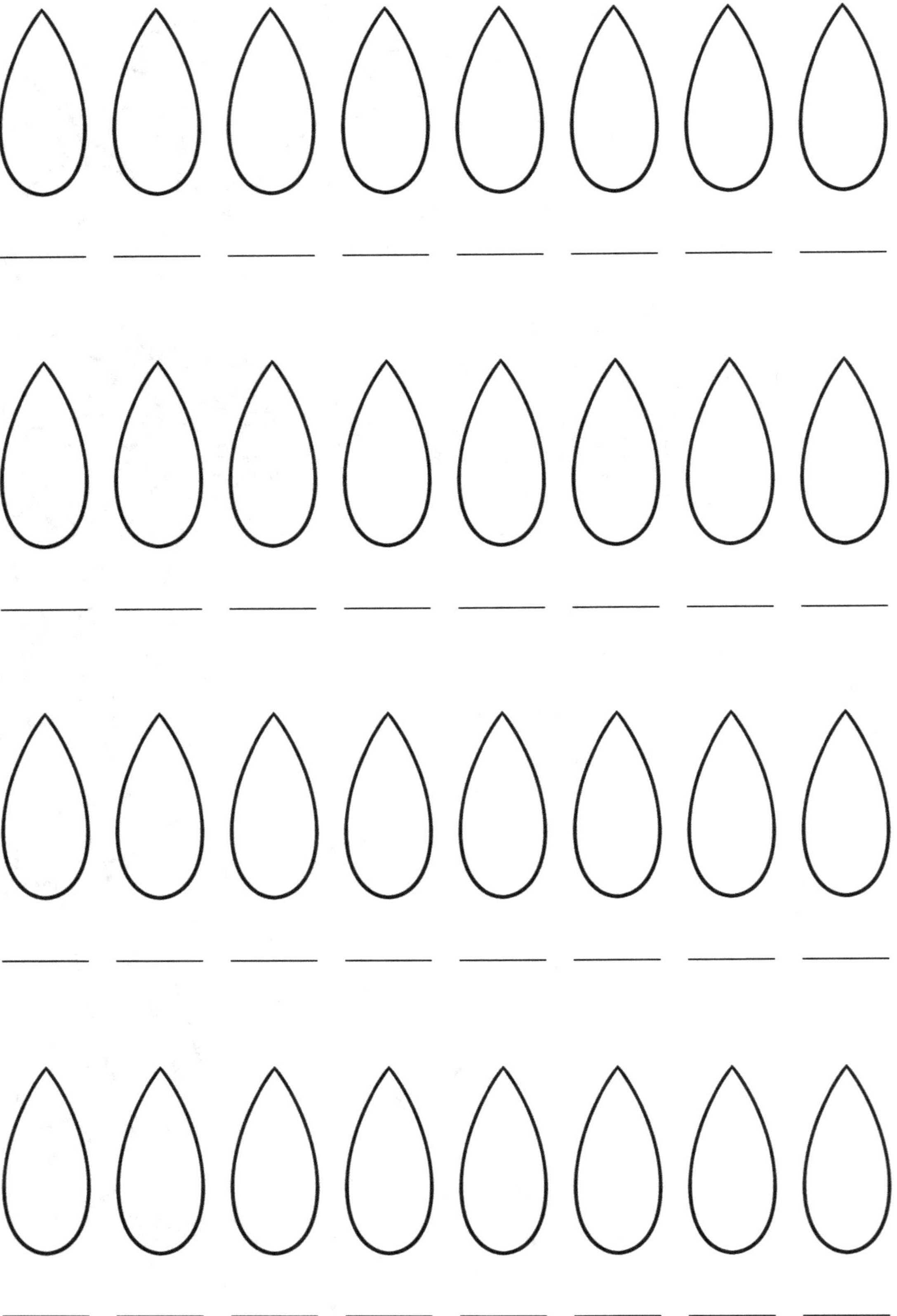

SWATCH YOUR COLOURS

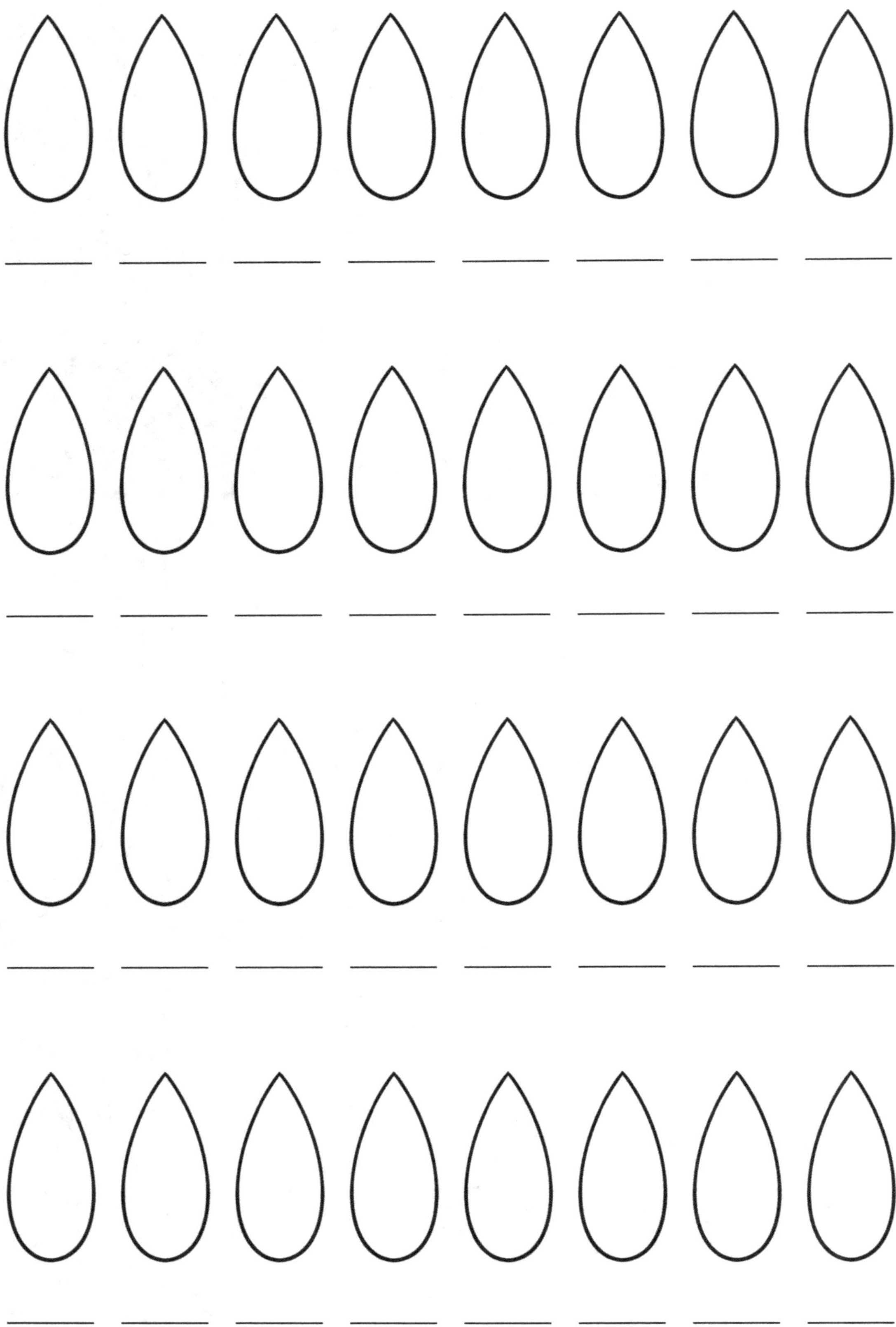

SWATCH YOUR COLOURS

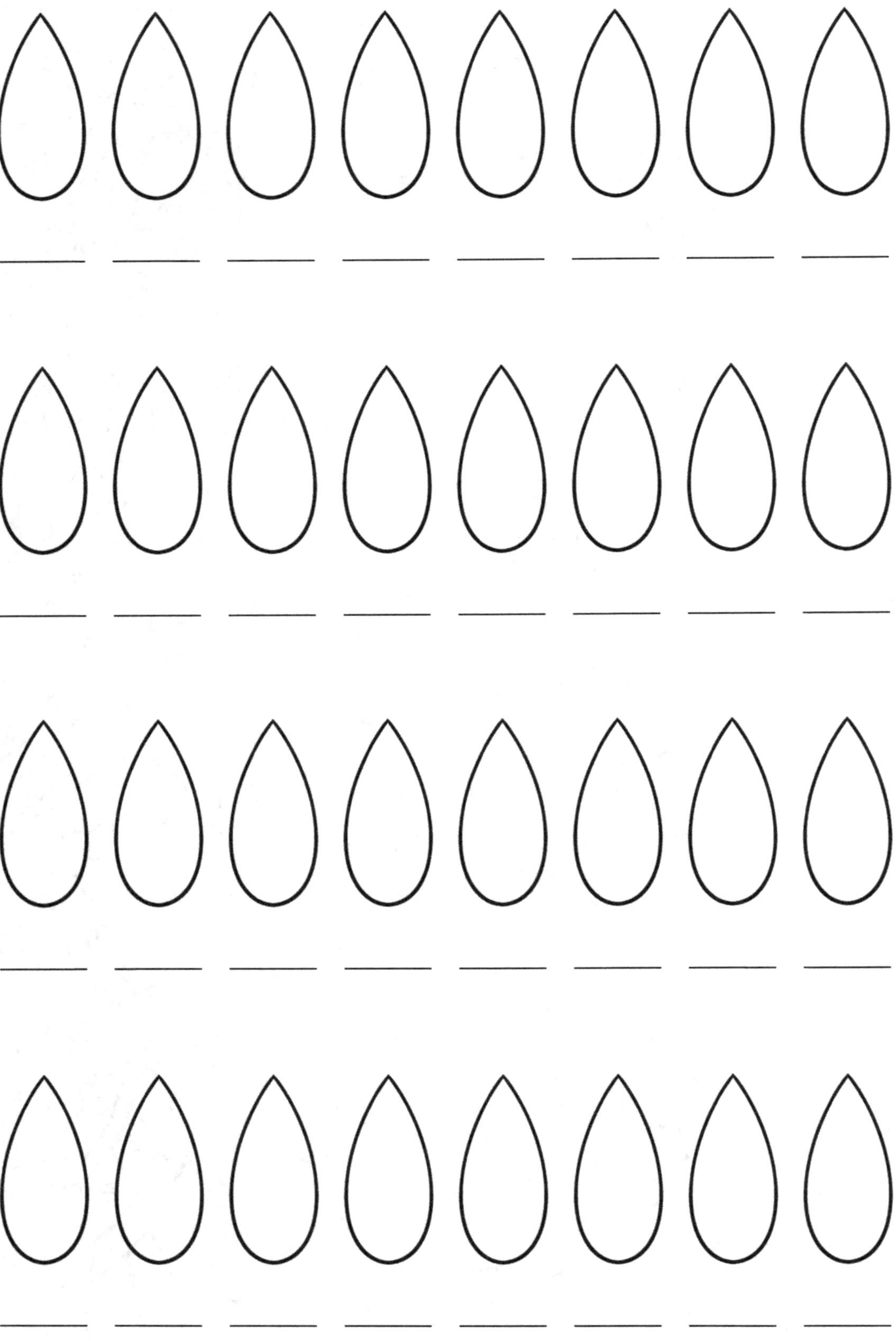

SWATCH YOUR COLOURS

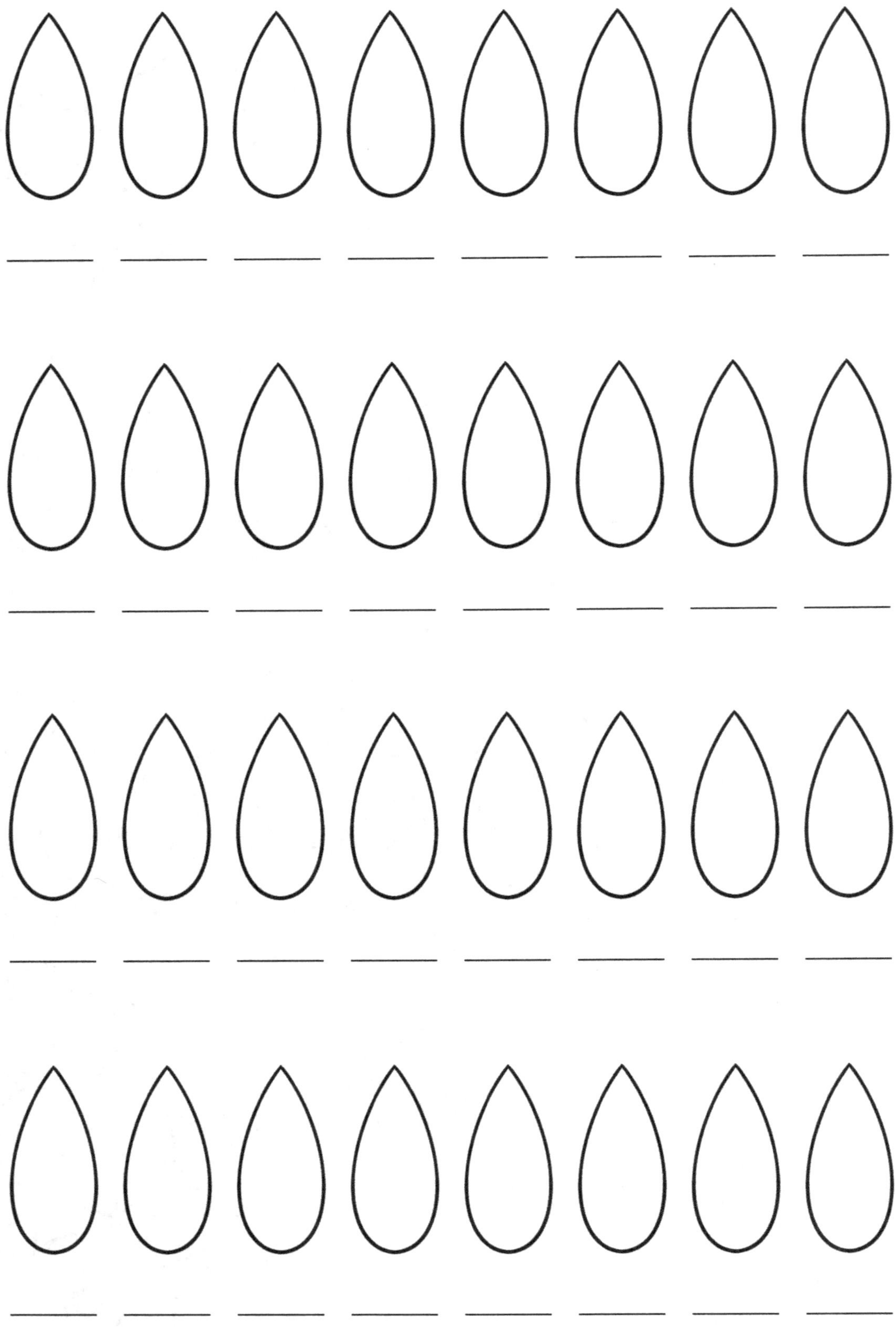

SWATCH YOUR COLOURS

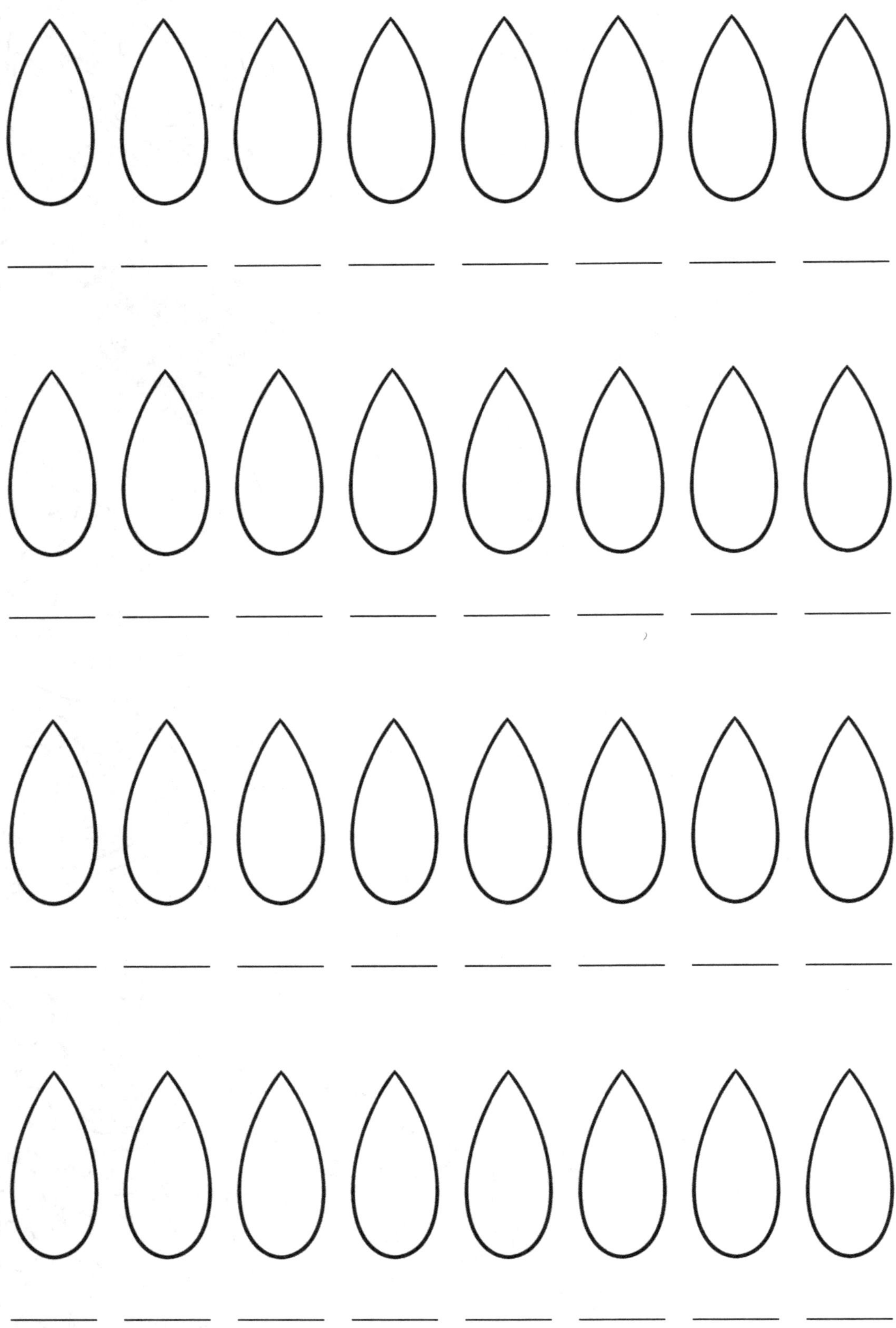

SWATCH YOUR COLOURS

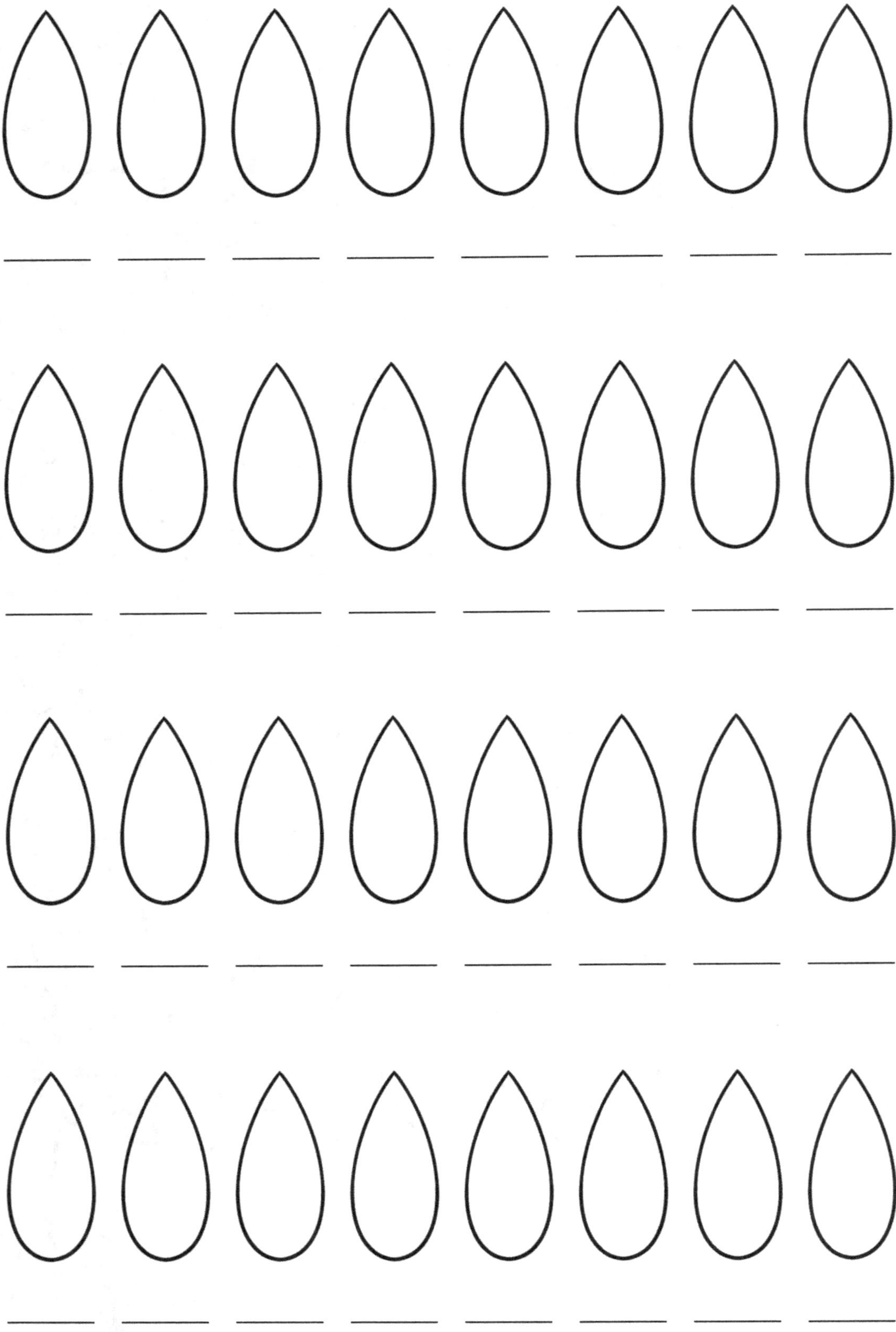

SWATCH YOUR COLOURS

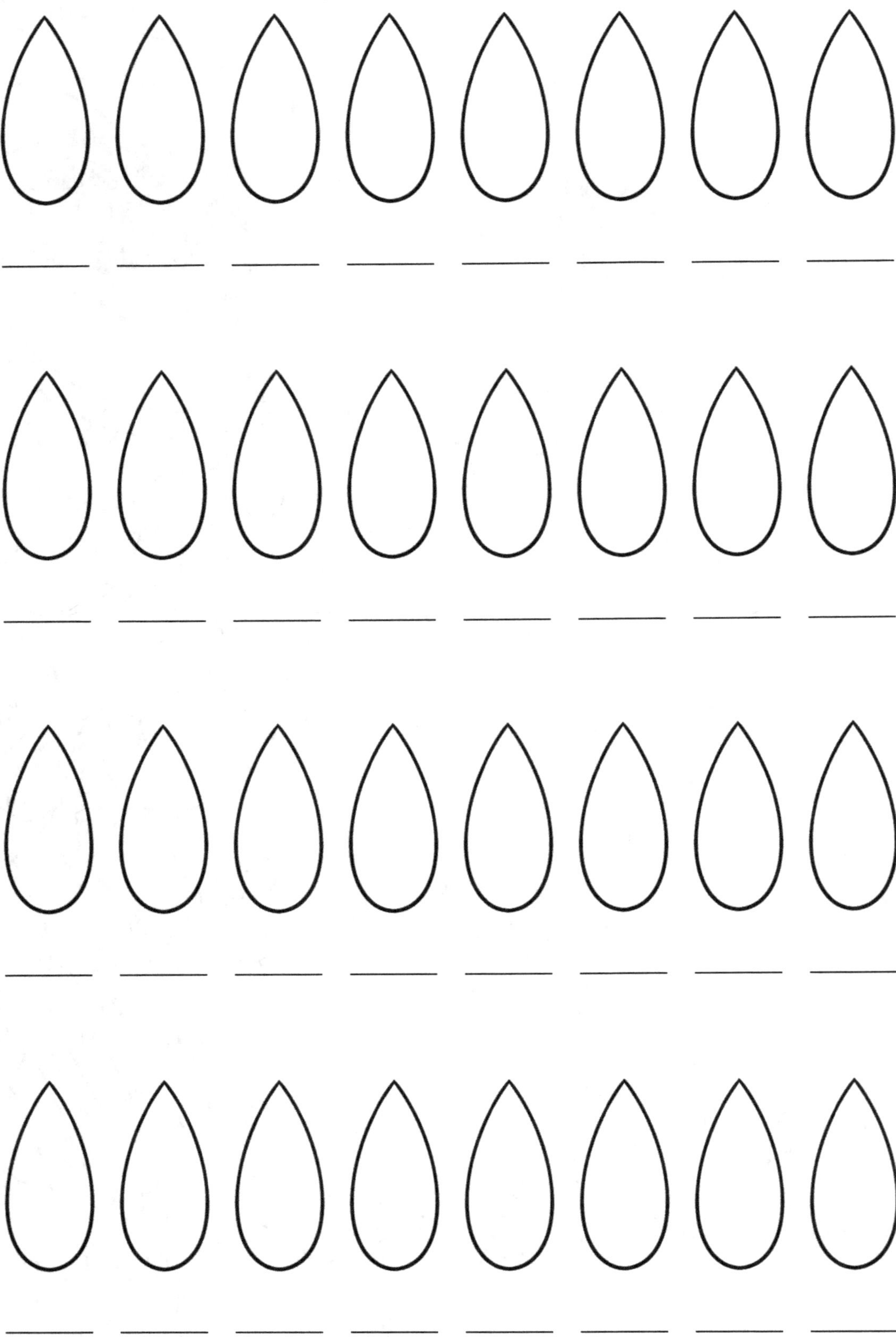

OWL TWO NIGHTER

SWATCH YOUR COLOURS

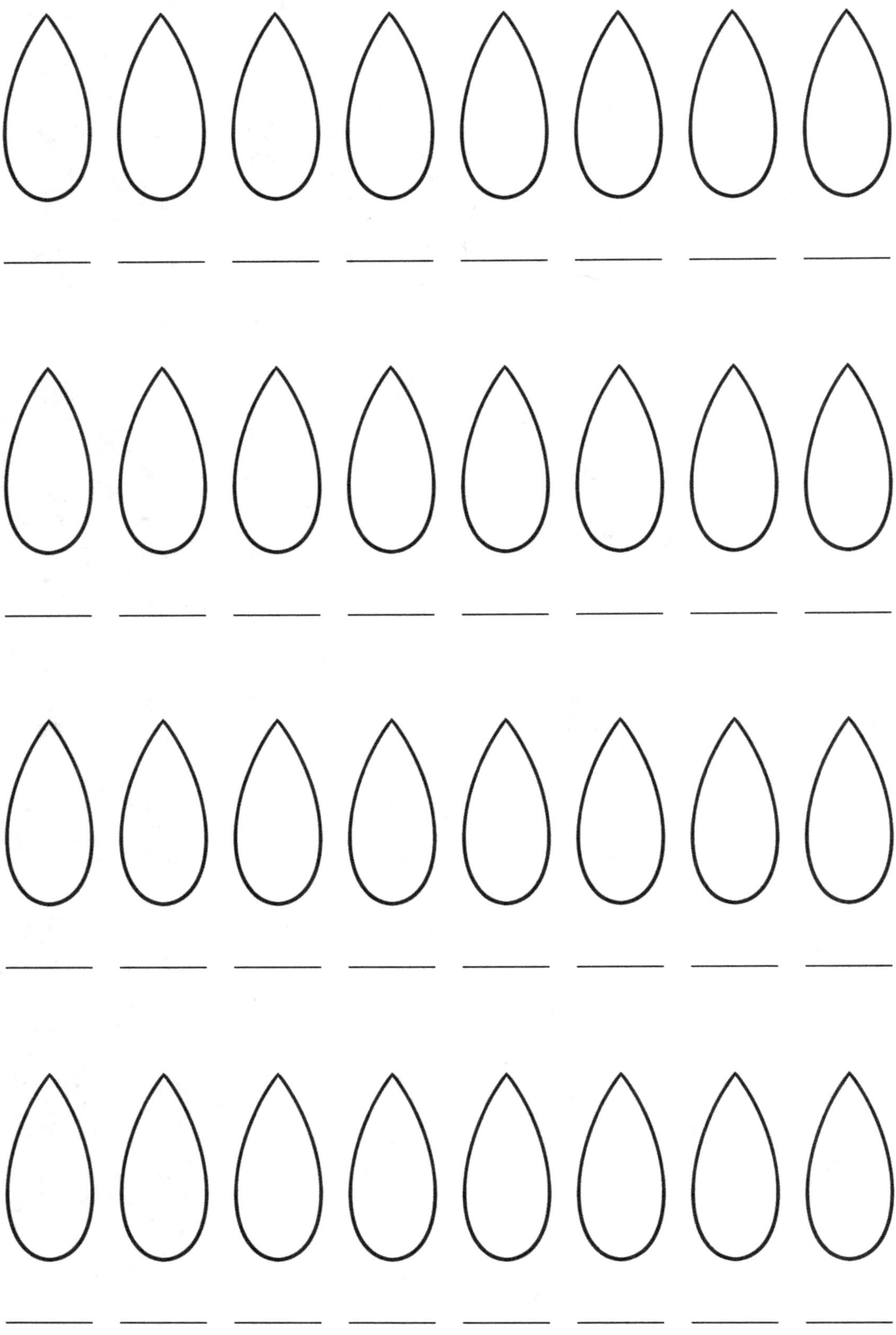

SWATCH YOUR COLOURS

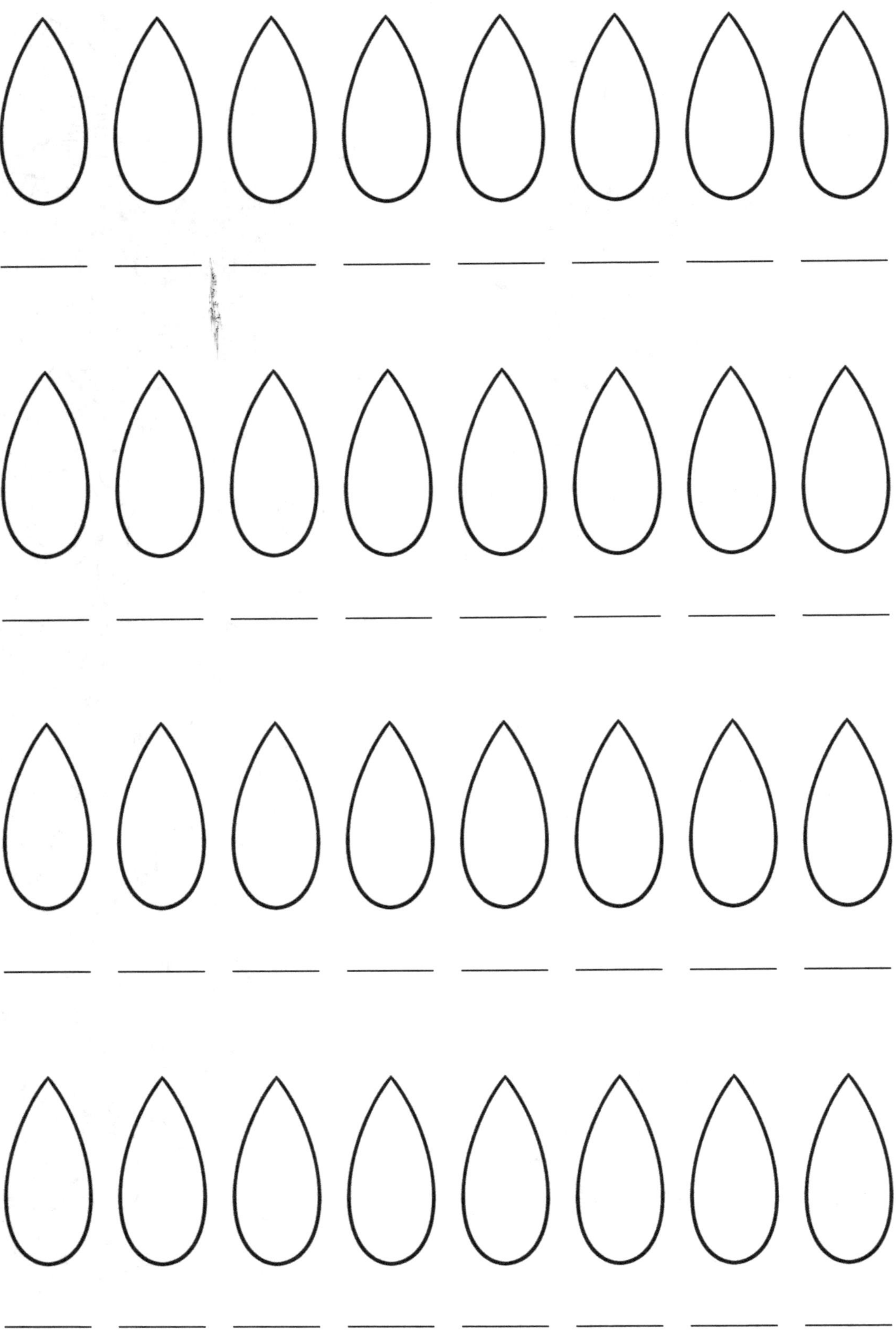

SWATCH YOUR COLOURS

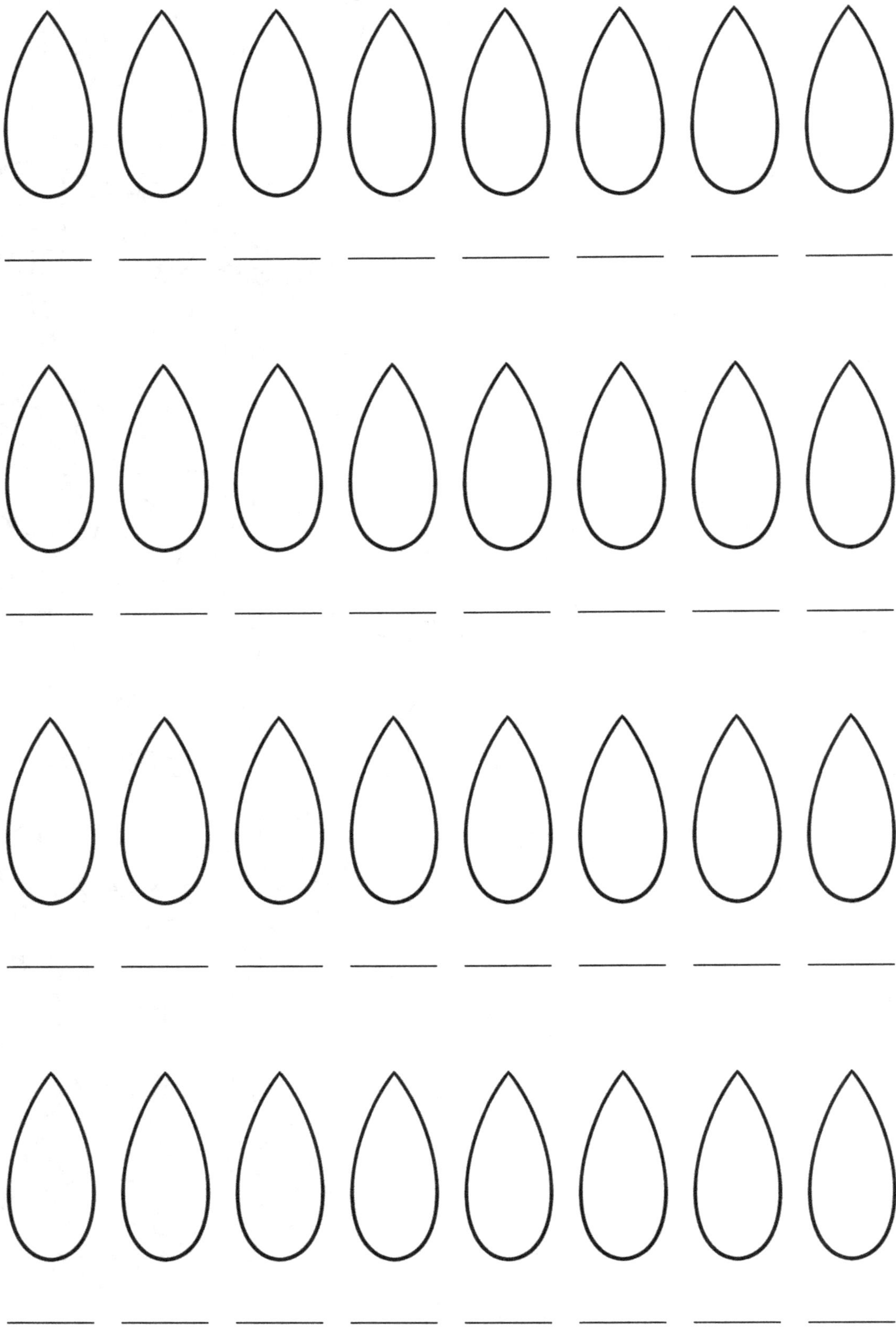

TWEET LOVER

SWATCH YOUR COLOURS

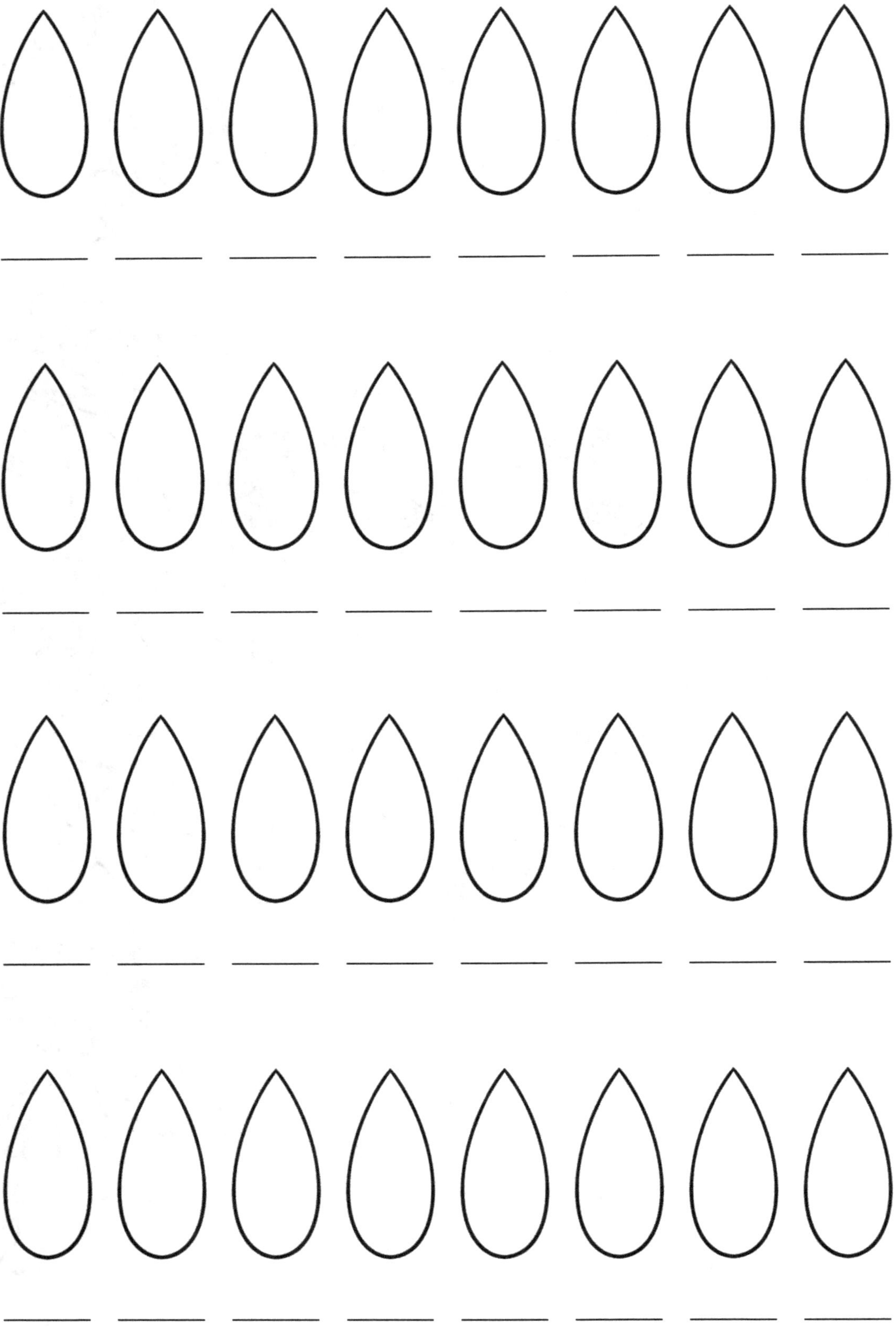

SWATCH YOUR COLOURS

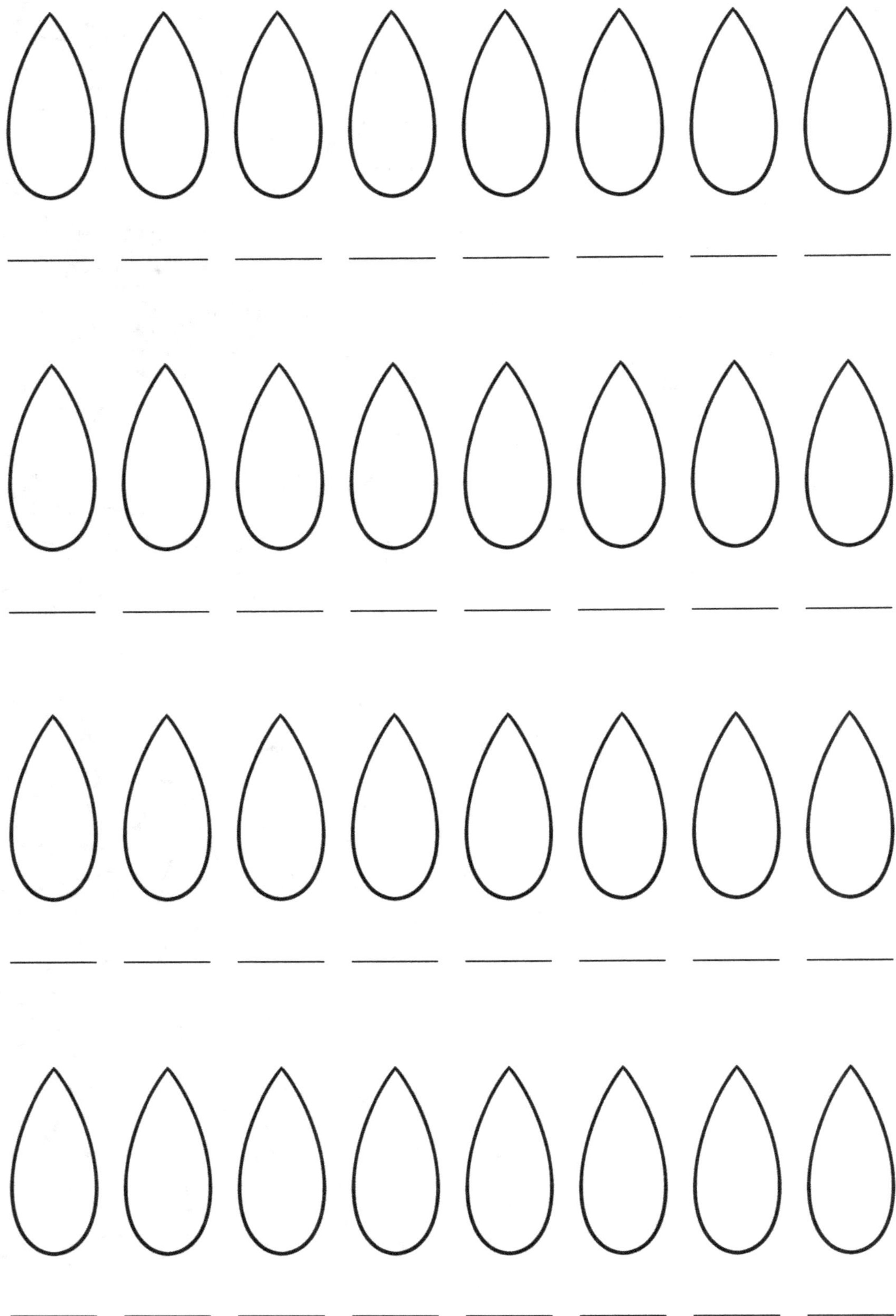

SWATCH YOUR COLOURS

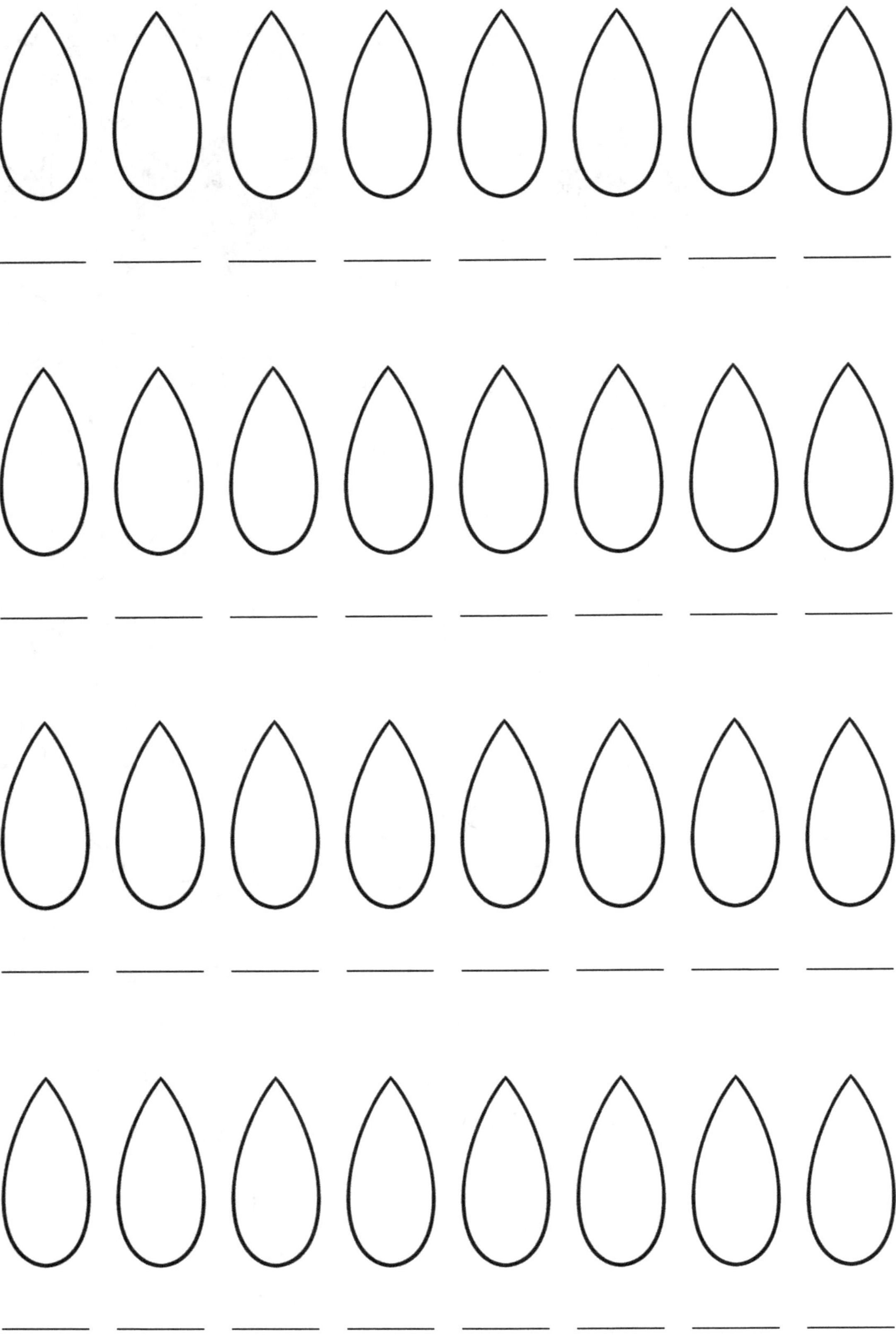

OWL INDEX

This is the Owl-Mazing collection of owl colouring pages inside this book.
You can use these tiny ones to mark off and date the ones you've finished, cut
them out and pop in a journal or if you're up for the challenge colour them too.

They'd definitely be cute, but not sure even I'd be up for that!

➔ GET YOUR COLOUR ON!

Then share your artwork on social with the world or just with me,
I love seeing your finished masterpieces!

You can tag me directly in your posts @_helloangel_
or use the tag #icolorwithhelloangel

Check me out on www.Facebook.com/HelloAngelCreative
and join the Hello Angel colouring group Hello Angel Colouring Stars.

If you just want to share with me send it in an email to helloangelart@gmail.com

But most importantly just enjoy your colouring time xx

9 781705 387603